a SAVOR THE SOUTH *cookbook*

Crabs & Oysters

a SAVOR THE SOUTH *cookbook*

Crabs & Oysters

BILL SMITH

The University of North Carolina Press CHAPEL HILL

Library of Congress Cataloging-in-Publication Data
Smith, Bill, 1949 January 11–
Crabs & oysters / Bill Smith.—1 [edition].
pages cm.—(Savor the South cookbooks)
Includes bibliographical references and index.
ISBN 978-1-4696-2262-0 (cloth : alk. paper)
ISBN 978-1-4696-7759-0 (pbk. : alk. paper)
ISBN 978-1-4696-2263-7 (ebook)
1. Cooking (Crabs) 2. Cooking (Oysters) 3. Cooking, American—
Southern style. I. Title. II. Title: Crabs and oysters.
TX754.C83S65 2015   641.6′95—dc23
2015006183

To the memory of all of those
glorious meals we had at the beach and to
the people who cooked them

Contents

a SAVOR THE SOUTH *cookbook*

Crabs & Oysters

Introduction

egend has it that the author Colette's system had become so delicate by the time she died that she could
have only oysters and champagne. I hope this happens
to me.

I grew up in eastern North Carolina catching crabs,
cleaning fish, and shucking oysters. I loved the beach. Still do.
Today when I look back, the best memories I have of those times
always include something to do with food and the beach. In the
summer, my family and I would often go down to the beach after
church and spend the day, and even though we only lived thirty
minutes from the ocean, we would still take a beach cottage for at
least a week sometime in July or August. The ocean and the coast
were so much a part of our lives that we never really considered
going anywhere else. People from eastern North Carolina are like
that. I hope to share some of this vibe with you in the recipes here.

When I was five or six years old, I would go on Sunday afternoon "rides" with my father's brother, Alex, and his wife, Hi. These
excursions usually included lunch. One of our favorite places was
a seafood restaurant in the town of Sea Level in Carteret County.
On one such afternoon, I ordered soft-shell crabs. My aunt Hi
was sure that I had meant deviled crabs, but I wouldn't change
my order. (Deviled crabs are mildly spicy crabmeat baked in the
crab's shell. Soft-shell crabs are the whole beast minus the face
and the guts, fried crispy, and eaten shell and all.) She ordered
deviled crab just in case. When lunch came, she had in fact been
right. I had meant deviled, but of course I wouldn't admit it and
the rest is history. To this day soft-shell crabs are one of my favorite foods.

Part of my family is Roman Catholic, so Fridays put seafood on
the table every week. This was in the days before Vatican II when
meat was forbidden to us on that day as a small bit of penance.

1

Fridays were "fish days." A strange idea of punishment I thought to myself, but then I've always been impious.

In New Bern in the 1950s our two rivers were lined with "crab factories." These were small crab-packing houses where you could buy crabs and crabmeat. Mostly, though, we caught our own with chicken necks tied on string. All you had to do was slowly coax the crabs near to the surface of the water and scoop them up with a net. They were ridiculously easy to catch. Crabs were essentially free food. We learned to clean and pick them ourselves.

Oysters were more often gifts. My father worked for the post office, and for a time his route was in rural and maritime Pamlico County, which has a long coast of marshes and bays. In those days people gave gifts to the mailman, so besides the piña colada cakes, corn, or homemade sausage, we sometimes received a bushel of oysters. Strangely, oysters will keep out of the water, under wet burlap, in a cool, dark place for a long time. I remember baskets of these in our basement. The health department says never to do this, of course. (See the instructions for storing oysters later in this chapter.)

We learned early to eat them roasted. Backyard oyster roasts were held in good weather. People built permanent pits, not for barbecue, but for oysters. You soon learned to dodge the smoke and not to burn your fingers as you helped yourself. You could of course have raw oysters as well. At oyster parties, my uncle Alex would delight and terrify us at the same time by also eating the tiny crabs that either scurry out of freshly shucked oysters or don't out of roasted ones. These tiny "pea crabs" were once a commercial product. In the March 20, 1893, edition of the *New York Times* there is reference to an oyster crab salad.

I have retained the *r*-month prejudice against eating oysters in warm weather (that is, oysters should be eaten only during months that contain the letter *r*). It's the way we were raised, I guess, plus by summer they have become too big for my taste. Having said all this, I always eat them when I'm in New Orleans whatever the time of year or whatever their size. It's almost always warm there, and a trip to Casamento's is always in season.

This is a southern book by definition, and the South has a long seacoast. Nine of the states of the old Confederacy have shore-lines. Add in Maryland (some do, some don't) and there is a lot of ground, or perhaps water, to cover. And so while North Carolina will figure heavily in this work, I've looked all over the South for things to include. A large part of what I've discovered has been found in church and community cookbooks. I've come to feel that these are the true repositories of southern cooking culture. This research has been delightful, and I have learned a great deal more than I would have imagined at the start. I will never forget how to spell Worcestershire, for instance. It is in everything. There are a host of sensible but forgotten techniques that come up again and again in these old books. Several people use a double boiler rather than a skillet to soften peppers and onions before they are incorporated into a dish. Beurre manié, used to thicken or finish sauces, shows up a lot. You rarely see it called for today, although it works like a charm. Sometimes the descriptive language is too good to be true. "Take a knob of butter the size of a walnut . . ." comes to mind.

I became the chef at Crook's Corner in 1993. Besides cooking, the job requires a surprising amount of travel, especially around our region, and hence I have gotten to spend lots of time in both Charleston and New Orleans, the South's two most sophisticated bastions of good food. I've also had the pleasure of visiting the Eastern Shore Virginia to meet fisher folk, and of spending a morning on the docks in Dare County, North Carolina, hearing people talk about their work. This book became both academic and hands-on.

I had planned to organize these recipes by course—from soup to nuts, as it were. It turns out that a lot of these things aren't so easily categorized. We serve both oyster stew and fried oysters as first courses at Crook's, but both could be a main course. I've included a new (for me) slaw recipe that's good with the fried oysters, in case you decide to do that. Pickled oysters are often served at cocktail parties, but again at work, I've been tossing them with roasted beets to make a salad. A few of the crab salads could be used as the main course for a light luncheon. Oyster dressing is a side dish. Fortunately, I didn't discover any desserts using either crabs or oysters, but I did come up with a beverage or two. Two are for real and come from Mexico, and the other is a strange sort of tonic from the early 1900s.

Before we begin cooking, there are some technical things to address. Some of them deal with health and safety. Some of them have to do with the vocabulary of the trade, others with the seasonal nature of our subjects.

Let me start out by saying that health department officials are a lot more skittish about seafood than I was raised to be. We learned certain commonsense precautions growing up, but by and large anything we caught we ate right away or froze for future use.

The strictures regarding crabs are much less alarming than those concerning oysters. The National Restaurant Association's course book on food safety advises that crabs must be sold alive and kept cool and moist. Processed crabmeat should come from reliable sources, kept at 41°, and used within the recommended time period.

All fresh seafood must be kept cold, usually directly on ice. Never eat crabs that have died after you bought them alive. Don't eat oysters raw that you haven't seen shucked—or at least know who did it and when. When you shuck them yourself, they should be difficult to open. Only buy from reputable fish markets. Smell will tell you a lot, as will appearance. Soft-shell crabs should have plump, lustrous gills, for instance. Even the guts you squeeze out of them should smell fresh and oceanic. The condition of the waters from which these creatures are taken must be considered as well. There are many places where I fished as a child that are unappetizing today, to say the least. Crabs present a little less worry since they are almost always eaten completely cooked. Oysters, on the other hand, involve more peril not only because they are eaten raw or partially cooked but because of the filtering nature of their feeding. Otherwise wholesome oysters may have ingested something unpleasant. There is the possibility that they've accumulated dangerous toxins or harmful organisms. Both of these problems are the result of the condition of the waters where the oysters live. Store live oysters at 45°. The opinion of the food inspection community is that it is never ever completely safe to eat raw or barely cooked oysters. Harmful bacteria *can* be killed by cooking thoroughly, but there are certain toxins not detectable by smell or taste that are not destroyed by either cooking or freezing.

Again, the bottom line is to buy from reputable seafood merchants who know where their products have come from. Having said all this, though, I decided long ago to keep eating oysters until one of them gets me.

Grades of Crabs and Oysters

An important point to note right away is that the crab in this book is the North American blue crab — *callinectes sapidus* — the "beautiful swimmer." This is the crab native to the southern coast. There are 4,400 species of crab in the world, and according to *The Encyclopedia of Food*, all of them are edible. Processed blue crabmeat comes in grades according to the part of the animal from which it comes. It is usually sold by the pound, and a pound of crabmeat goes a surprisingly long way. Jumbo lump is far and away the most expensive grade. It should be made up of the two large pieces of meat that are on each side of the animal where the outside legs attach to the body. Regular old lump contains some of the smaller chunks in the same region of the animal. Back fin is next. This is a mixture of all of the body meat. It usually contains a lump or two right on top for the buyer to see. Claw meat is next, coming, in fact, from the arms and claws. Lastly is something called special, which comes from the whole body. It tastes fine and is made up mainly of shredded meat. It is a good value and is especially good for dips and soups, as long has it has been properly cleaned. A sort of separate category is something called cocktail claws. These are claws that have been cracked and shelled but with the meat intact and the point of the claw left on as a handle. They are usually sold in one-pound cartons. These would seem to be a lot of work to prepare, so it is odd that they are usually inexpensive. As far as I know, crabmeat is always sold pasteurized, i.e., cooked. Obviously, the rule about eating dead crabs does not apply here. Every recipe here that uses crab starts with the instruction to pick through it carefully for bits of missed shell. Soft-shell crabs are blue crabs that have just molted. The crab grows but its shell does not, so in the spring they shed their hard shell and are briefly entirely edible. Right before this happens, they are known as peelers. Crabbers watch for crabs at this stage and move them to shedding tables and wait. If left alone, the soft crab's new shell would harden up in a day or so. With the crab kept out of the water, this hardening is slowed down. It used to be said that crabs begin to shed at the full moon in May, but in recent years it has begun earlier than that. Consecutive warm nights are the trigger, and these now begin to happen in April. Soft-shells are generally sold in cardboard trays lined with either straw, seaweed, or damp newspaper and come in five sizes, although I believe that the classification of "medium" is not legal to catch and keep in all jurisdictions: mediums are 3½-to 4½ inches; hotels, 4½–5 inches; primes, 5–5½ inches; jumbos, 5½–6 inches; and whales (or whalers), 6-plus inches.

Hard crabs seem to be graded by industry consensus. The most desirable is the #1 Jimmy crab. This is the mature male. All crabs are graded into five sizes: small, 5–5½ inches; medium, 5½–6 inches; large, 6–6½ inches; jumbo, 6½–7 inches; and colossal, 7-plus inches. The minimum size for harvesting is 5 inches "point to point." The other types of classification are: #2 Jimmies, which are less meaty and sometimes have just shed. They are usually sold to crab-picking companies. #3 Sooks are mature females. #4 Sallys are immature females. Sponge crabs are mature females that are carrying eggs, or roe, under their aprons. The roe is added to she-crab soup. Live crabs are sold by the piece or the bushel. The number of crabs in a bushel will, of course, vary according to their size.

Whereas crab harvesting is somewhat self-regulating due to crabs' seasonal habits, oysters need some rules. Most state laws are broad guidelines that leave the details to their fisheries departments. In North Carolina the season is roughly from mid-October to early May. There are private beds that have slightly different rules. Harvested oysters must be at least three inches long from hinge to lip. Oyster sellers must provide harvest tags that list the fisherman, the location of the oyster bed, and the date of catch, and these must be kept on file for ninety days. Restaurants that serve raw oysters must keep copies of these tags on premises for ninety days as well. Shucked oysters are generally graded standard, select, and extra-select. A pint of standard oysters will contain around twenty. Selects and extra-selects are progressively larger, and thus the number in a pint will go down. Remember that it's best not to eat these shucked oysters raw, although I have done it and survived. When I purchased shucked oysters for these recipes, I always got selects. If you shuck your own, you will usually get a variety of sizes, but unless they are really huge, you should be able to proceed as instructed here.

Oysters in the shell are sold either by count or by bushel. The number in a bushel will, again, depend on the size, but generally a bushel weighs around fifty pounds. Research turned up claims of from 100 to 200 oysters per bushel, so you'll need to ask when you buy. They can be very muddy. The best way to really wash them is out in the yard with the garden hose.

People are surprised to learn that virtually all of the oysters in eastern North America are the same species—*crassostrea virginicus*. So whether they're called Wellfleets, Blue Points, or Beausoleils, they are all the same animal. They are sort of like dogs, I guess. The differences in shape, size, saltiness, and flavors are the result of locale, or "meroir," as people are fond of saying these days.

Cleaning Crabs

I have been cleaning crabs all my life, but describing it to someone else without having one in hand is difficult. Unless you can persuade your fish market to clean them for you, you must start with live crabs. Some people have to stop right there. Fishing is really the last instance where you have to kill what you eat. I got over this years ago.

SOFT-SHELL CRABS

Soft-shell crabs are less of a problem than hard-shell crabs because they can't hurt you.

1. Take a crab in one hand, holding it right-side-up in the middle of its back with the face pointed away from you. I use just my thumb and index finger to hold them.
2. Using kitchen shears, clip off the eyes. This means cutting off what would be the face. You want to get both the eyes and the mandible beneath them but as little else as possible. I think the only reason this is done is because people don't want to have dinner staring at them.
3. Lift both the pointed sides of the shell up to reveal the gills. These look like a row of soft fangs. Snip these away.
4. Cut away the tail flap. This is underneath the back of the crab. Males have a narrow flap, females a wide one.
5. Under running cool water, gently but firmly squeeze out the yellow and grey soft matter that is found just underneath the shell. Try to do this without breaking the crab.
6. Rinse thoroughly, allowing the water to run underneath the shell and inside of each crab.
7. Place on a clean kitchen towel in a place where they can drain; cover with crushed ice if you are using them right away, or refrigerate them for later use. They can also be frozen. Carefully wrap each crab in several thicknesses of plastic wrap. Try to make time to thaw them slowly in the refrigerator when you want to cook them.

HARD-SHELL CRABS

Hard-shell crabs will fight back. Although you can easily snap a claw off with two fingers, they have enough strength to hurt if they can get to you first. If possible, put them in the freezer for twenty minutes before cooking or cleaning them. This renders them all but dormant. Sometimes, though, when you have a crowd to feed, this won't be practical. For my father's eightieth birthday party we made crab stew for sixty people, and suddenly I was the only person who remembered how to clean live crabs. There was no freezer large enough to hold this many, so I was on my own in the back yard. In any case, cleaning crabs is best done outside with a garden hose at hand. Hope that there won't be many mosquitos and that you don't kick over your beer. Crabs usually come in bushel baskets and often cling to one another, forming long, squirming chains. Shake them apart as best you can.

1. Grasp each crab in the same way you did the soft ones, with the face pointing away from you. You will soon learn how to stay out of their reach.
2. Coming in from behind, snap off the claws with your fingers.
3. Working quickly, pull off the back shell. It will usually come off in one piece. (Save these if you are making deviled crabs.) This will again reveal the gills and something called the devil's fingers or sometimes dead man's fingers.
4. Before cleaning out this part, I chop the bodies in two down the middle with a cleaver or large knife. There is a line on the belly to guide you. This finishes the kill.
5. Under running water, using your fingers, shears, or a paring knife, clean away the innards. At certain times of the year you will also find bright orange "coral" or roe. This can be saved to enrich sauces or soups. Its color makes it obvious and easy to extract. I never count on finding this, and if I use it, it is usually an afterthought.
6. Rinse the crabs well and set them on towels to drain for a bit. Then either put them in crushed ice to be used soon or cover and refrigerate to use later.

You can also freeze crabs once they are cleaned. Wrap each one very well in plastic wrap. I'm not crazy about frozen crabmeat, but these will be fine for stewing. If you have saved the crab backs for deviled crabs, rinse them in cool water and then cook them in boiling water for seven minutes. Cool them in ice water, then drain. They will keep for a while in the fridge.

Alternately, when you need crabmeat but only have live crabs, toss them into a large pot of boiling water as you would a lobster. There is no nice way to do this. The water should be salted and if you like, seasoned with seafood boil. You are salting for the amount of water, not for what is cooked in it, so taste before you add the crabs. If necessary, cook them in batches in order not to crowd them. When the crabs are bright red (no more than ten minutes depending on size), stop the cooking by transferring them into ice water. Drain as soon as they are cool since it's not good to soak them in water indefinitely.

Picking the meat takes patience. Pull off the back shells and save the pretty ones if you are making deviled crabs. The best meat is found where the legs join the body in the part of the crab that would be the tail. This is where the largest "lumps" are, but there is meat throughout the whole body, as well as in the claws. I use kitchen scissors and a nut pick to get at it. It takes a dozen large crabs to yield a pound of crabmeat.

Cleaning and Opening Oysters

Cleaning and opening an oyster is a lot less complicated than cleaning crabs.

1. Begin by cleaning the shells. This helps prevent sand or bits of shell from getting into the meat. Again, the best tool for this is a garden hose with good pressure, but you can, of course, do this in the sink. Most people who sell oysters in the shell give them at least a preliminary rinse.
2. Put them in the sink under cool running water and go over each one quickly with a scrub brush. You will never get them spotless but can remove most of the loose grit. Use an old dish towel to help you hold each oyster firmly. This also helps protect your hand from cuts either from sharp edges the shells may have or from the oyster knife you are wielding in the other hand.
3. For opening oysters, I prefer a knife designed for this purpose. Kitchen knives are too sharp and too flexible, and

you will be more liable to stab yourself with them. Oyster knives are short, blunt, and sturdy. Turn the oyster so that the deep side of the shell is on the bottom. This will allow the juice to collect in the deepest side of the shell.

4. Holding the oyster in one hand, insert the blade of the knife into the hinge of the oyster and wiggle it in as far as it will go. Twist the blade with force. Sometimes the shell will give suddenly, so be careful not to jab yourself. (Oysters vary wildly in size, shape, and structure. Some have shells that are more brittle than others.) Keep wiggling the knife as you force the shell open. Take your time until you get the knack of it. If you do enough of this, you will eventually develop skill and speed.

5. Once the oyster is open, wipe the knife blade before you proceed so as not to introduce any grit inside. Muscles attach the oyster to both sides of its shell. One is much stronger than the other. Use the knife blade to sort of scrape and sever both of these so that they become detached from the shell, while trying to reserve the juice.

6. If you are not eating the oysters as you go, collect them and their juice in a clean bowl and refrigerate. Try to use them within twenty-four hours.

Oyster shells are good for the garden. All over eastern North Carolina they are piled up around the root of fig trees for fertilizer. When that need is filled, they are used to pave driveways. These days there are also recycling programs that collect them for creating new reefs for growing more oysters.

One caveat about cooking oysters *in* things: When they are cooked, they release an unpredictable amount of juice, or liquor, as it is also called. Sometimes it's a lot, sometimes not. This can play havoc when you are trying to thicken things. If you end up with too much juice, sometimes you can correct this by adding more of the thickening agent. Other times, reducing the liquid (by cooking it longer) might be preferable, but if you do this, remove the oysters first. Set them aside until your sauce is correct, then stop the cooking and return the oysters to the dish.

I've tried to sort the following recipes in a logical way, but as I said earlier, their place on the menu is changeable. Circumstance, season, and custom can come into play and change the norm. It would not be unusual to be invited to an oyster roast that included only oysters and beer, and that would be great. So much for courses. As you read and use this book, keep in mind that my intention was to entertain as well as to instruct. It was fun to include recipes that on the surface seem a little silly in this age when people are always sitting down to "a serious dining experience." You see, I was raised to see every meal as a little party.

Hors d'Oeuvres

Hors d'oeuvres are often served to guests before they sit down at the table, as something to nibble on until everyone arrives or something to have with drinks. Likely as not they are finger foods, so if they seem at all messy, make sure there are plates and napkins at hand.

Deviled Crab Dip

This delicious little recipe is as simple as can be, and you're likely to have all the ingredients except for the crab in your kitchen any time.

MAKES 10 OR SO SERVINGS

½ pound fresh special crabmeat, picked over for shell
3 hard-boiled eggs, chopped
½ cup mayonnaise
1 tablespoon fresh lemon juice
½ teaspoon dry mustard
½ teaspoon onion powder
½ teaspoon salt
⅛ teaspoon black pepper

Carefully fold all of the ingredients together, taking care not to break up the crab too much. Cover and chill for at least 1 hour. Serve with Ritz crackers.

Crab and Artichoke Dip

The real sweep of the internet was made plain to me when I decided to do a little investigating about this ubiquitous recipe. The minutiae are endless. The varieties are endless. No crab cookbook can be without it. Generally, these dips are baked and then brought to the table hot from the oven. Sometimes they are kept warm in chafing dishes, but they can become oily if they sit too long over low heat, so it is perhaps better to make them in small batches to be heated as needed. This amalgam contains Ritz crackers, but these same crackers are often recommended as the thing to be dipped as well. Although this dip has come to be seen as somewhat pedestrian, I find this version rather luxe. It will work very well for a cocktail party that overlaps dinner time. I didn't try to break up the artichoke hearts at all. This made it more of a spread than a dip. Thick, well-toasted garlic bread would be a better vehicle than crackers.

MAKES 10 OR SO SERVINGS

1 (13½-ounce) can quartered artichoke hearts, well drained

¼ cup mayonnaise

10 Ritz cracker, crushed by hand

2 tablespoons chopped pickled jalapeños

½ cup freshly grated Parmesan cheese

½ teaspoon fresh lemon juice

¼ teaspoon Worcestershire sauce

½ pound fresh back fin crabmeat, picked over for shell

Lemon wedges

Garlic toast

Preheat the oven to 320°. Combine all the ingredients but the crabmeat and put in an attractive oven-safe serving dish. Bake for 20 minutes or so or until hot and beginning to brown. Remove the dish from the oven and quickly stir in the crab with as little mixing as possible to keep the meat somewhat intact. If it seems too dry, stir in a few more tablespoons of mayonnaise as well. Return to the oven and cook for 5 minutes more to warm the crab and to make the top pretty again. Bring to the table. Serve with lemon wedges and garlic toast. This is actually really good cold the next day.

Dot's Crab Dip

My aunt Dot loved to entertain. At her house she always had a pot of coffee waiting should you drop by. She also always set out little buffets of snacks at holidays. I found this recipe in my father's collection. It calls for commercial French salad dressing. I have always thought that there was a place for commercially prepared products in my menu. I would never try to make Girl Scout cookies, for instance, and where in the world would we be without Tabasco sauce?

MAKES 10 OR SO SERVINGS

4 tablespoons unsalted butter, softened
½ pound fresh special crabmeat, picked over for shell
½ cup grated sharp white cheddar cheese
1 tablespoon prepared horseradish
4 tablespoons bottled French dressing

Carefully mix all the ingredients together and chill, covered, for at least 1 hour. Serve with—you guessed it—Ritz crackers.

Pickled Oysters

I love pickled shrimp, but I had never had these until I began working on this book. There are many recipes from eastern North Carolina but I never encountered them growing up. There are three schools of thought here. Some recipes say to cook the oysters in their own juice and then put them, drained, into vinegar brine. Another recommend cooking them straight away in the brine. The oysters really didn't survive this well. The third had you dump the oysters, juice, and all into the brine. This was too watery for me. Here, I adopted the first method. People serve these at cocktail parties with just toothpicks and napkins, but at Crook's Corner we've turned them into a salad by tossing them with roasted beets (recipe follows).

MAKES 1 QUART

---

1 quart shucked select oysters with their juice
1 cup vinegar
6 whole cloves
6 bay leaves
1 (at least) hot pepper pod (fresh or dried)
1 teaspoon celery seeds
¼ teaspoon ground mace
1½ teaspoons salt

Bring the oysters to a simmer in their own liquid over medium heat and cook just until they begin to curl. At the same time, bring the vinegar to a boil with all of the seasonings in a non-reactive (i.e., enamel or stainless steel) saucepan. Strain the oysters and stir them into the vinegar. (You might save the broth for a soup or stew.) Immediately remove the pan from the heat and set it in ice to stop the cooking. Refrigerate overnight before serving.

Roasted Beets

I use red beets mostly, but keep in mind that their color will over-whelm anything you mix them with. This amount makes enough to turn the Pickled Oyster recipe (page 19) into a salad course.

MAKES 2 SERVINGS

4 peach-size beets
2 teaspoons olive oil
2 bay leaves
4 whole cloves
1 teaspoon whole fennel seeds
½ teaspoon salt

Preheat the oven to 350°.

Put the beets in a bowl with the oil and the seasonings. Swirl everything around and put it in to a baking dish. Cover tightly and place in the oven. Check after 40 minutes by piercing a beet with a knife. If the knife passes easily through the center, the beets are done. If not, you should be able to judge how much more time will be needed for them to finish cooking (see Note). When they are done, allow them to cool in their own juice. Peel them when they are cool enough to handle. Slice into rounds, then cut the rounds into ¼-inch-wide strips. Chill.

Toss together with the drained oysters. Add a little of the oyster brine and taste for salt. Serve as a salad.

NOTE ✳ Beets can vary a great deal in terms of how long they should be cooked. Some are dense and slow to cook, while others cook as quickly as a baked potato. The same goes for peeling: some can be peeled by rubbing them with a dishcloth, while others will require a paring knife. I have never been able to tell which kind I have before I cook them.

Crab-Stuffed Eggs

This is a fancy and substantial version of deviled eggs that I found among my grandmother's recipes. I've taken a few liberties here. Hard-boiled eggs are an excellent platform for all sorts of elaborate snacks. It is generally thought that there can never be too many deviled eggs. This recipe uses only a dozen.

MAKES 24 DEVILED EGGS

12 hard-boiled eggs
½ cup mayonnaise
1 teaspoon yellow mustard
¼ teaspoon salt
⅛ teaspoon black pepper
½ pound fresh special crabmeat, picked over for shell
2 tablespoons diced pickled jalapeño
A mixture of equal parts chili powder and smoked paprika
    to decorate the tops

Slice the eggs in half lengthwise and scoop out the yolks into a bowl. Mash them with a fork and then stir in the mayonnaise, mustard, salt and pepper. Carefully fold in the crab and pickled jalapeño. Fill the egg whites and dust tops with the paprika mixture.

Two Crab-Claw Cocktails

On a trip to New Orleans once, I noticed little dishes of crab claws were being served almost everywhere we went. When I asked about them, my friend Charles said that there isn't really a recipe for them—everyone has their own. Sometimes they are hot, sometimes cold; sometime spicy, sometimes not. A pound carton usually contains around three dozen shelled claws. One carton will serve at least four people. Here is a hot version and a cold version.

Crab Claws with Basquaise Sauce

I guess that this sauce is really just a salsa with meat. I suppose you could serve it with chips, and I've certainly eaten enough of it by itself. It needs to be cold, but don't try to make it too far in advance as it begins to lose its crunchiness after a time. This is also a good sauce for the Roasted Oysters (page 61).

MAKES 4 SERVINGS

1 carton crab claws
5 strips bacon, chopped raw, or 1 cup side meat, diced
Two celery ribs washed and diced (save and chop the leaves
    if they are pretty)
½ medium green bell pepper, diced
½ small red onion, diced
2 tablespoons diced pimientos
Zest and juice of 1 lemon (I like to use a zester that
    makes threads for this)
Chopped fresh herbs
1 cup good-quality olive oil
Salt and black pepper, to taste

Brown the bacon in a large skillet. Drain the bacon, leaving a little of the grease in the pan and cool it enough so that it won't cook the other ingredients. Stir in the rest of the ingredients and season with salt and pepper. Arrange the crab claws on 4 dishes with the shell ends sticking up. Spoon the dressing over them and let them sit for half an hour before serving. Rough chop the celery leaves and sprinkle on top at serving time.

Crab Claws St. Charles

You don't really need to do anything to cocktail claws if you don't want to. Just squeeze a lemon wedge over them and eat them right out of the box. If you want to be fancier than that, try this. Basically, the sauce is the snail butter used by the French to make escargot. Make sure you have bread on hand to mop up the leftover sauce once the claws are gone.

MAKES 4 SERVINGS

1 carton cocktail claws

1 stick unsalted butter, softened

Juice and grated zest of 1 lemon

3 large cloves garlic, minced

½ cup fine, toasted bread crumbs

1 tablespoon chopped fresh parsley

1 teaspoon coarse sea salt

Preheat the broiler.

Inspect the claws for bits of shell. Arrange them in 4 oven-proof ramekins, with the shell ends sticking up; set aside.

Put 2 tablespoons of the butter in a small skillet and warm it. As soon as the butter melts, stir in the bread crumbs and then the garlic. Turn up the heat and cook until the garlic sizzles and smells good, being careful not to let it brown. Add the lemon juice all at once. Put the skillet in the refrigerator for a minute or two until it has cooled down enough to touch.

In a small bowl, mash the rest of the butter with a fork; add the garlic mixture, lemon zest, and parsley and thoroughly combine. Add the salt, mixing just until incorporated—you want the crystals to remain whole. Refrigerate the composed butter to allow it to firm up.

Crumble a tablespoon or so of the composed butter over each ramekin and broil until the butter is sizzling and a little browned, about 8 minutes, more or less, depending on the effectiveness of your broiler. Serve at once. Any leftover butter freezes well and will have a million uses.

Soups and Stews

Soup is a natural destination for crabs and oysters.
Here are a few nice recipes, but I suspect that the list
of them is legion.

Crab Bisque

Bisques made from lobster or shrimp often start with the shells. Oddly, I didn't come across any crab bisque recipes that called for that, but if you are starting with whole crabs, you might use some of the boil for this recipe if it's not too salty. Most recipes seem to be very timid when calling for the sherry or Madeira. I am not.

MAKES 4 VERY ELEGANT SERVINGS

4 cups milk, divided
1 tablespoon all-purpose flour
4 egg yolks
1 pint heavy cream
1 cup fresh crabmeat (grade of your choice),
    picked over for shell
¼ cup plus 4 teaspoons sherry or Madeira, divided
Salt and cayenne pepper, to taste
4 teaspoons unsalted butter
Paprika

Bring 3 cups of the milk to a simmer in a double boiler. In a Mason jar with a lid mix the flour into the remaining cup of cold milk. Shake vigorously to make as smooth as possible. When the milk in the pan has started to bubble around the edges, strain the flour mixture into it through a kitchen sieve, whisking constantly.

In a small bowl, whisk the egg yolks and cream together completely, then whisk in a cup of the hot milk. Through the sieve, strain this slowly back into the rest of the simmering milk, stirring all the while until the mixture is hot, being careful not to let it boil. Stir in the crabmeat and ¼ cup of the Madeira and season with salt and cayenne.

To serve, put a teaspoon of butter in the bottom of each of 4 bowls. Ladle in the soup. Top each with a sprinkling of paprika and 1 teaspoon of the remaining Madeira.

Soupe Hendaye

This recipe comes from my days at La Residence, Bill and Moreton Neal's wonderful and, if I may opine, groundbreaking restaurant here in Chapel Hill. Bill encouraged the cooks to think of the kitchen as a "laboratory." We worked primarily with French classic recipes, but we were given permission to occasionally stray. Hendaye is the southwesternmost town in France on the Spanish border. The name was chosen because the soup is in the Basque style. We would sometimes use commercial seafood broth if we didn't have the fixings for homemade.

MAKES 6 SERVINGS

---

3 bell peppers (of various colors, if possible)
1 small red onion
½ cup dry white wine
2 quarts seafood broth, at room temperature
1 pint shucked select oysters with their juice
Salt and black pepper, to taste

Under the broiler, in a very hot oven, or on a grill, roast the bell peppers whole. They will eventually collapse and the skin may char a little. The time this takes will vary. A grill is faster than most broilers, which in turn will be quicker than an oven. The moisture content of the peppers is also a factor. Over the flames of a grill, 5 minutes on a side should be enough time. The same under an open flame broiled. Electric broilers will take more time, but you need to watch. Put them in a paper bag and allow them to sweat for half an hour. Peel and clean them under cool running water. Seed and cut into narrow strips. Cut the onion into similar strips.

Pour the wine into a soup pot, and turn the heat to high. Stir the broth and oyster juice together and whisk into the warming wine. Bring the broth to a simmer.

Skim the broth of any unsightly foam. Add the onion and cook for about 15 minutes, then add the peppers. Your soup is now ready for the oysters. Just before serving time, add the oysters to the simmering broth. Cook them just until they begin to curl, a minute at most. Season with salt and lots of pepper.

Corn and Crab Chowder

I've been a fan of this soup ever since I first had it in 1969 at a drugstore lunch counter in a small town on the coast of Maine. ("Maine?" you ask.) For the most part, while testing these recipes, I've used commercially packed fresh crabmeat. You can, of course, catch and pick your own crabs. Twelve large crabs yield about a pound of meat. When making soups, you have the extra bonus of being able to use the boil for stock. When I first starting making this soup, I finished it with heavy cream (as chowders often are). Later I just allowed the potatoes to dissolve a little, thickening the soup, and decided not to add any. Both versions are great. I have used commercial clam juice as part of the liquid in this soup as well.

MAKES 6–8 SERVINGS

¼ pound side meat, diced

1 small onion, peeled and diced

2 tablespoons cornmeal or Maseca (instant corn masa flour)

4 cups water (or 4 cups of your crab boil)

3 baking potatoes, peeled and diced

2 cups corn cut from the cob, cobs reserved

¼ teaspoon crushed red pepper flakes

3 bay leaves

1 pint heavy cream (optional)

Salt and black pepper, to taste

½ pound fresh special crabmeat, picked over for shell

Render the side meat in a heavy-bottomed soup pot. When it has begun to brown and to give up some grease, add the onions and cook until soft, about 5 or 6 minutes. Do not brown them. Stir in the cornmeal and cook for 3 minutes more. Whisk in the water and stir to smooth any cornmeal lumps. Bring to a simmer, then add the potatoes, corn, reserved corn cobs, bay leaves, and red pepper. Cook until the potatoes are tender, about 20 minutes. Fish out the corn cobs.

Whisk in the cream, if using, and bring the chowder back to a simmer. Taste for salt and pepper. (The side meat has been seasoned already with salt and pepper so you may not need more.) If the chowder seems too thick, add a little more water or crab boil (or cream). Fold in the crabmeat and cook for a few minutes more just to warm it. Serve at once.

Louis Osteen's Brown Oyster Stew

I first had this stew at breakfast on the last morning of a Southern Foodways Alliance Symposium in Oxford, Mississippi. I remember wishing that I had thought of it first. This has happened to me before with Louis's cooking. He was kind enough to let me reprint his recipe from his cookbook Louis Osteen's Charleston Cuisine.

MAKES 4 SERVINGS

4 tablespoons benne seeds
2 tablespoons peanut oil
2 tablespoons (about 1 ounce) very finely diced pancetta
   or side meat
2 tablespoons finely minced yellow onion
2 tablespoons all-purpose flour
1¼ cups heavy cream
24 shucked oysters, juice strained and reserved
1¾ cups seafood stock (store-bought is fine)
1 teaspoon chopped fresh thyme
1 tablespoon fresh lemon juice
1 teaspoon sesame oil
2 tablespoon chopped fresh chervil or Italian parsley,
   or a combination of both
Salt and freshly ground black pepper, to taste
Buttered toast or oyster crackers

Place the benne seeds in a small, heavy-bottomed sauté pan over medium heat and dry roast them by cooking them for about 9 minutes or until they become dark and fragrant. Remove from the stove. Roughly crush half of the seeds with a spoon.

Heat the oil in a heavy-bottomed saucepan over low heat. Sauté the pancetta or side meat for about 5 minutes or until crisp and lightly browned. Remove the meat with a slotted spoon and drain on a paper towel. Leave the oil and fat in the saucepan.

Add the onion and the crushed benne seeds to the saucepan and sauté for about 3 minutes, stirring frequently. When the onion is slightly browned, add the flour, stir well to combine, and cook for 2 minutes. Meanwhile, in a separate pan, heat the cream to just below a simmer.

Whisk the reserved oyster juice, stock, and thyme into the onions. Simmer and stir until there are no lumps. Add the warmed cream and simmer for 5 minutes more. Add the oysters, the uncrushed benne seeds, lemon juice, sesame oil, and herbs. Cook just until the oysters begin to curl. Taste for salt and pepper.

Serve in warm bowls garnished with the pancetta or side meat with buttered toast or oyster crackers on the side.

Cocktel

This is a cold soup that is often found in Mexican restaurants. It's a cross between gazpacho and a salad. In this version I've used only crabmeat, but I have seen it served with octopus, oysters, and shrimp. The "deluxe" version of this is often finished with a can of Orange Fanta. Skip that part.

MAKES 6–8 SERVINGS

---

1 (46-ounce) can tomato juice
1 large green bell pepper, seeded and diced
1 medium red onion, diced
2 celery ribs, diced
2 (or more) jalapeños, finely diced
1 large avocado, peeled, seeded, and cubed
Juice and grated zest of 1 orange
1 tablespoon fresh lemon juice
½ pound fresh crabmeat (grade of your choice),
    picked over for shell

Combine everything except the crab and chill until very cold. At serving time, fold in the crab.

Sit-Down First Courses

The recipes in this section are for occasions that are a little more formal—that is, you'll want a fork and a place to sit. An aspic cannot be eaten when you are standing around a campfire. The last two recipes could be the main course at a light lunch.

Corinne Dunbar's
Artichoke and Oyster Cocktail

I salute any recipe that calls for a quarter of a stick of butter per person. This is an unusual recipe in another regard. It serves only one. I can imagine curling up in a window seat and eating this out of an antique soup cup on a cold winter afternoon.

This recipe comes from Cooks from Old Brook *(Brookhaven Junior Auxiliary [1982]), a cookbook that I received as a gift over twenty years ago. It was published by the Junior Auxiliary of Brookhaven, Mississippi. The present members of the chapter voted to allow me to reprint it. It is one of the best of these locally publish books that I've seen.*

I love this recipe, but it is sort of ugly. I sprinkled it with some chopped mint leaves to brighten it up. Any fresh herb except cilantro would work, I think.

MAKES 1 SERVING

---

1 small artichoke
4 large oysters
2 tablespoons unsalted butter
1 teaspoon Worcestershire sauce
Salt and black pepper, to taste
Chopped fresh mint or another favorite herb (optional)

Boil the artichoke in salted water until done, about 16 minutes. (A sharp boning knife should pass easily through the thickest part of the base.) Stop the cooking by submerging it in ice water for 2 or 3 minutes. Set it upside down on a towel to drain for a minute or two more. Scrape the leaves and cut up the heart. Place the artichoke with the rest of the ingredients in the top of a double boiler and cook just until the oysters begin to curl. Serve hot.

Oysters in Champagne

This recipe came from my late friend Henry Hobbs. He was also from Mississippi and was the father and grandfather of several good friends. He was a large, urbane, witty man and I always enjoyed his company.

You can buy shucked oysters to make this, but then you won't have the shells to use as serving dishes. Also, you don't need to be extravagant when purchasing the wine. Any nice, clean-tasting one will do, but if you go too far down the list, the reduced wine will have a nasty nose. You'll need to work quickly and have everyone ready to eat these. Poached oysters don't sit well for long. If you are not comfortable cooking so many of these at once, it is fine to cook and then bring them to the table in smaller batches.

MAKES 6 SERVINGS

3 dozen oysters, well-scrubbed and rinsed

3 cups champagne or other sparkling wine

4 tablespoons unsalted butter

1 generous teaspoon curry powder (hot or mild,
   according to your preference)

2 tablespoons chopped fresh parsley

Salt and black pepper, to taste

Shuck the oysters and save them in their juice. Rinse the shells and reserve the deeper half of each one. (You can do this much in advance.)

When you are ready to eat, put the empty shells in a hot oven. Put the champagne in a large skillet or wide-bottomed saucepan and bring to a gentle simmer. Arrange the warmed shells on a platter or on plates. Gently slide the oysters into the simmering wine along with a half cup or so of their juice. Cook them just until they begin to curl a little, a minute max. Put 1 oyster into each warmed shell.

Turn the heat to high and quickly whisk in the curry and butter. Whisk vigorously and allow the wine to reduce and thicken just a little. Season the oysters with salt and pepper. Add the parsley to the sauce and spoon a little over each oyster. Serve at once. Serve with champagne, of course, and any of the leftover broth. Toast Colette.

Crab Aspic

OK, OK, aspic is the joke food of southern cooking. Stuffy ladies' luncheons spring to mind. It's one of those dishes that shows up all the time even though everyone claims to dislike it. It is the fruitcake of the salad world. This recipe is an amalgam of two—one from my aunt Theresa and the other from a friend of hers from church. I tried to taste this with a dispassionate tongue and have decided that I like it. I also wonder now why everyone makes fun of these. But then I also like fruit cake.

It's best to make this a day ahead if you can so you will be sure that the mold has set completely. The original instructions called for a "decorative ring mold." I didn't have one of those so I used a one-quart porcelain loaf pan. This is probably lucky because I have vague memories of decorative ring molds that wouldn't release their contents evenly, leading to irritated panics on the part of hostesses. Whatever you use, dip a paper napkin in cooking oil and coat the pan completely. You don't want it to be greasy, but you must cover every bit of it. Put the mold in the refrigerator to chill.

One of the recipes suggests serving this in "lettuce cups." If you do, slice the mold using a thin, sharp knife; dip it in very hot water each time since the crabmeat can be uncooperative.

MAKES 6 SERVINGS

- ½ pound fresh crabmeat (grade of your choice), picked over for shell
- 2 envelopes (1½ tablespoons) gelatin
- ½ cup cold water
- 2¼ cups tomato juice
- ¼ cup cider vinegar
- 1 teaspoon Worcestershire sauce
- 1 teaspoon fresh lemon juice, plus a little grated rind
- 1 teaspoon prepared horseradish
- ½ teaspoon salt

Pinch or 2 of cayenne pepper

1 teaspoon Tabasco sauce

1 tablespoon seeded, minced jalapeño pepper
   (about half a pepper)

½ cup minced celery

5 martini olives, thinly sliced into rounds

1 cup mayonnaise spiked with ½ teaspoon paprika and
   ¼ teaspoon chili powder

Set the crab in a sieve to drain. You will discard any liquid. Dissolve the gelatin in the cold water. Bring 1¼ cups of the tomato juice to a simmer in a nonreactive saucepan, then remove from the heat. Whisk the gelatin into the juice and then stir in the remaining juice and the vinegar. Whisk in the Worcestershire sauce, lemon juice and rind, horseradish, salt, cayenne pepper, and Tabasco.

Set the pan, uncovered, in the refrigerator to cool for at least 1 hour. Stir from time to time. Just before the gelatin is completely set up, it will pass through a stage that resembles a runny jelly. This is when you fold in the vegetables and the crab. Use a spatula and distribute the ingredients evenly. Turn into the oiled loaf pan. Return to the refrigerator and allow to set, overnight if possible.

To unmold, set the aspic mold in a pan of hot water that will come ¾ of the way up the sides of the mold for 2 or 3 minutes. This will slightly melt the edges, allowing the gelatin to come free. At the same time, gently loosen the mold from the edges using your fingers. Remove the mold from the water and dry the outside of it. Place a serving platter on top and quickly flip the mold, giving it a few sharp shakes as you do. The salad should emerge jiggling and glistening. Return it to the refrigerator to recover.

You may either bring the salad to the table as a piece or slice it into individual servings. Top with a dollop of the seasoned mayonnaise.

Oyster Fritters

I've deliberately avoided recipes that call for ground or minced oysters—and there are more of them than you would think. Here is the exception. In Belhaven, North Carolina, there was a famous inn called the River Forest Manor. Its buffet was legendary. The dish most often mentioned was the oyster fritters. I couldn't find that recipe, but this reminds me of it. I've added corn as recommended in another recipe that I came across from Maryland. When really hot, these fritter almost don't need any sauce, but I've included a tartar sauce recipe for good measure (page 46). Make the tartar sauce in advance and put it in the refrigerator so it can set up a little. It'll be good with other things in this book as well.

MAKES 3–4 DOZEN

---

6 large shucked oysters, drained and roughly chopped

1½ cups all-purpose flour

1 teaspoon salt

⅔ cup milk

4 eggs, separated

1 tablespoon cooking oil, plus more for frying

½ cup cooked corn kernels (frozen is fine or use leftover corn on the cob)

Sift the flour and salt together into a large bowl. Add the milk and mix well. In a separate bowl beat the egg yolks with the oil and then beat into the batter. Beat the egg whites with a pinch of salt to stiff peaks and fold by thirds into the batter. Combine the oysters and the corn and carefully fold them into the batter. Let rest for half an hour in the refrigerator to "cure."

Fill a straight-sided saucepan with 4 inches of oil and heat the oil to 365°. (If you don't have a thermometer, you can test the temperature with fair accuracy by dropping a few specks of the batter into it. If the oil is ready, the batter will sizzle, float, and brown quickly.) Working in batches, drop the batter into the oil by tablespoons. Don't crowd. When the bottoms get a little brown, 2 to 3 minutes, turn the fritters and cook until this side is also brown. Remove to a dish covered with paper towels and continue cooking the rest of the fritters. You will need to stir the mixture from time to time as the corn and oysters will settle to the bottom. Mostly these work, but every once in a while a fritter will fall apart in the oil. I ate these fragments as I cooked for everyone else. If too many fall apart, tighten the batter with a little more flour. (See the comments about oyster juice on page 11.)

Tartar Sauce

2 cups mayonnaise
¼ cup drained and roughly chopped capers
¼ cup chopped fresh parsley
¼ cup minced scallions, green and white parts
3 garlic cloves, minced
½ cup chopped pickles or drained pickle relish
2 tablespoons Dijon mustard
2 teaspoons grainy mustard
2 tablespoons whole mustard seeds, quickly toasted
   in a dry skillet
1 teaspoon dry mustard
2 tablespoons fresh lemon juice
Pinch of cayenne pepper

Mix everything together and chill.

Crabmeat Salsa

My Mexican friends have been feeding me variations of this for years, only instead of crabmeat, they use either canned tuna or raw hamburger—really. We eat it on fried tortillas, but it is easy to imagine it spooned over black beans and rice. Of course you can buy ready-to-eat chips for this, but warm, just fried tortilla wedges bump everything up a notch.

MAKES 4 CUPS

---

2 large ripe tomatoes, diced into ¼-inch pieces
1 large onion, diced into ¼-inch pieces
2 jalapeños, or more to taste, finely diced
Juice and grated zest of 1 lime
3 tablespoons good-quality olive oil
¼ cup chopped fresh cilantro
Pinch of salt
1 cup fresh crabmeat (grade of your choice),
    picked over for shell
Salt and black pepper, to taste
Fresh tortillas or store-bought tortillas chips
Cooking oil for frying

In a medium bowl, toss the tomatoes, onions, and jalapeños with the lime juice and zest, oil, cilantro, and salt. Let the mixture sit in the refrigerator, covered, for half an hour. Fold in the crab, trying not to break it up too much. Season with salt and pepper.

Fan the edges of the stack of tortillas as you would a deck of cards so that will separate easily. Cut the whole stack into sixths. Fill a straight-sided saucepan with enough oil to float the tortilla wedges and heat the oil to about 360°. Working in batches so as not to crowd them, fry until crispy and brown. Drain them for a second in a sieve or on a towel and then toss with salt.

Serve the salsa with the warm tortillas.

Crab and Shrimp Calas
with a Riff on Tartar Sauce

I first had calas (rice fritters) in New Orleans the summer before Katrina. My friend Poppy Tooker, a Louisiana food writer and radio host, served them at a meeting of the Southern Foodways Alliance. Calas are a traditional street food but they had begun to disappear. It is Poppy's mission to save them from passing out of memory and being lost. On this morning, she served a sweet dessert variety.

*Jump forward eight years. Another friend, Lolis Elie, was promoting a cookbook (*Treme: Stories and Recipes from the Heart of New Orleans*) based on his TV series* Treme. *At the party we threw when he came to Chapel Hill, I wanted to serve at least one thing from that book. He and Poppy had by then come up with a savory version of calas, and this is based on their recipe. They used crayfish. I used crabmeat and shrimp for the party. They are so easy and so good that they are on my menu all the time now. I have been enlisted to Poppy's cause.*

Make the sauce first since the sour cream will need a while to recover its consistency. Grating martini olives is tedious, but for this delicious sauce it is worth it. My admiration for grated onion grows daily.

MAKES 3–4 DOZEN

FOR THE SAUCE
½ small onion, grated
½ small unpeeled cucumber, grated
6 martini olives, grated
2 cups sour cream
Salt and black pepper, to taste

4 cups cooked rice

12 scallions, both green and white parts, roughly chopped

¾ cup all-purpose flour

½ teaspoon salt

4 teaspoons baking powder

4 eggs, well beaten

1 cup fresh crabmeat (grade of your choice),
      picked over for shell

1 cup boiled shrimp, well salted, cooled, and roughly chopped

Cooking oil for frying

To make the sauce, put the onions, cucumber, and olives into a sieve, sprinkle with a little salt, and drain for about 10 minutes. In a small bowl, combine the sour cream with the vegetables and season with salt and pepper. Set the bowl in a bowl of ice and chill in the refrigerator for half an hour so that the sour cream can set up again. (Make a sandwich from the unused cucumber half, since it won't keep.)

To make the calas, put the rice in a large mixing bowl. Purée the scallions in a food processor until almost liquid and fold into the rice. Combine the flour, salt, and baking powder and stir into the rice. Fold in the eggs, followed by the seafood. Let the batter rest in the refrigerator for half an hour.

Using a small ice-cream-style scoop, form the batter into 1-inch balls. Fill a straight-sided saucepan with enough oil to float the calas and heat it to about 360°. (If you don't have a thermometer, you can test the temperature with fair accuracy by dropping a few specks of the batter into it. If the oil is ready, the batter will sizzle, float, and brown quickly.) Place as many calas into the oil as you can without crowding them. As they cook, they will float and brown. Usually they will turn themselves over as they cook; if not, do this with tongs. Fry for 4–5 minutes. Break one open to make sure they are done through. Serve hot with the sauce.

Crabmeat Remoulade

There was once a wonderful, old-school French restaurant on the East Side of Manhattan called La Cote Basque. The walls were painted with big murals of St-Jean-de-Luz. Bobby Short always seemed to be having lunch there. It was there that I first saw sauce painting. In the 1970s La Cote Basque was a touchstone in New York for cooks in French restaurants everywhere else. One of the many things I loved to get there was a remoulade of crab. This was the mustardy sauce of classic French cooking, not the red spicier one of Louisiana. I don't have the original recipe, but this is a close approximation. It really needs nothing else except a lettuce leaf to perch on and perhaps an olive or two on the side. Be sure to eat the leaf as well. This sauce is hard to make in smaller amounts, so this recipe makes more than you will need for a pound of crabmeat, but it keeps well and is good on other things, like hard-boiled eggs, Belgian endive, or romaine hearts.

MAKES 4 SERVINGS

---

1 pound fresh jumbo lump crabmeat, picked over for shell
1 cup boiling water
1½ cups Dijon mustard
¾ cup fresh lemon juice
3 cups olive oil
1 tablespoon chopped fresh parsley
Salt, to taste
Lettuce leaves
Olives (optional)

Go over the crabmeat for bits of shell, but try to leave it in large pieces. Usually, each lump will have a small blade of soft shell that helps hold it together. You can remove this if you like, but growing up, I just learned to spit it out.

Put the water, mustard, and lemon juice in the bowl of a food processor. With the machine running, slowly drizzle in all of the oil. Mustard is often already salty, so taste for salt. Gently toss the crab with the some of dressing to just moisten it. Serve as described above.

Crabmeat Ravigotte

Ravigotte is a French term indicating refreshment. (In Quebec years ago there were advertisements for the soft drink 7-Up that claimed "Ce Ravigotte!") I found examples of this recipe from Louisiana and from the southern parts of both Mississippi and Alabama. It is indeed refreshing.

MAKES 4–6 SERVINGS

1 pound fresh lump crabmeat, picked over for shell
1 tablespoon fresh lemon juice
Salt and black pepper, to taste
1 tablespoon Worcestershire sauce
3 tablespoons olive oil
4 scallions, both green and white parts, finely chopped
½ teaspoon finely chopped garlic
4 heaping tablespoons mayonnaise
1 hard-boiled egg, grated
Lettuce leaves

In a medium bowl, combine the crabmeat with the lemon juice and season with salt and pepper. Let stand for 30 minutes.

In a separate bowl, combine the Worcestershire sauce, olive oil, scallions, garlic, and mayonnaise.

Divide the crab into serving portions on the lettuce leaves. Spoon some of the sauce on top of each serving. Garnish with the hard-boiled egg.

Either/Or

The two recipes in this section can be used either as an appetizer or a main course. A big plate of fried oysters is a fine dinner as far as I'm concerned, but both at Crook's Corner and at dinner parties, I've served smaller portions as a first course. The same is true for oyster stew. In case you decide to serve fried oysters for dinner, an excellent recipe for slaw is on page 92. Fried seafood and slaw traditionally go together in the South.

People are always whining about fried food in the South, usually because they think the breading masks the flavor of what's been fried. I have absolutely no patience with this. There is in fact a tradition of beloved and tasty commercial breading mixes here. The recipe below got its start in Louisiana, but that isn't the only place that loves prepared seafood breaders. Many of these products predate the onslaught of convenience foods that came at the end of World War II. Three milling companies in North Carolina that make them are over a hundred years old. Almost all of them contain yellow cornmeal or flour, wheat flour, and powdered eggs. Variations include the addition of cracker meal, onion powder, and various sweeteners. I tried several of these and liked them all. The flavors were familiar as well because they have always been used in seafood restaurants along our coast.

Traditional Oyster Stew

It amazes me that something this good could be so easy. The only variation I ever encounter is chopped scallions added right at the end. Although it seems odd to me now, as a child I was often given this when I was sick.

MAKES 4 SERVINGS

4 tablespoons unsalted butter
1 quart whole milk
1 pint shucked oysters with their juice
Salt and black pepper, to taste
2 tablespoons chopped scallions (optional)
Oyster crackers

Put a tablespoon of butter in the bottom of each of four bowls. Bring the milk to a strong simmer in a large saucepan. Gently stir in the oysters and their juice. Return the milk to a simmer but do not allow a full boil. When the oysters are just beginning to curl a little on their edge turn off the heat. A minute in the simmering milk should be sufficient for this. Season with salt and pepper, keeping in mind that some oysters are saltier than others. Divide the oysters among the four bowls, then fill each with the warm milk. Garnish each with scallions, if using. Don't forget the oyster crackers.

Fried Oysters

This recipe is a happy accident. When I come home from a trip to New Orleans, I try to make a quick pass through the French Market on my way to the airport to see what's what. On one such visit I grabbed up lots of those local brand-name products that Louisianans love but are not found anywhere else. One was a seafood breader. I used it to fry flounder. The box was already in the trash before I realized how delicious it was. I fished it out of the dumpster. It revealed that it contained corn flour instead of cornmeal, which is traditional here. Thanks to the Latino grocery store around the corner, the corn flour was eventually replaced by Maseca, which is corn flour milled especially for tamales. This improved the recipe even more. Because I love crust on fried foods, I always use self-rising flour in my breadings. It gives a good puff when cooking. I serve these with Basic Cocktail Sauce (page 63) or Tartar Sauce (page 46). Lately I've taken to Sriracha sauce stirred into mayonnaise until it is the color of Thousand Island dressing.

MAKES SNACKS FOR 4 OR DINNER FOR 2
(although I can easily eat a pint of oysters myself)

---

2 cups Maseca
2 cups self-rising flour
2 teaspoons coarse sea salt, plus more for dusting oysters
    after they are cooked
1 teaspoon freshly ground black pepper
1 pint shucked oysters, drained
4 cups, more or less, oil for frying
Lemon wedges

Combine the flours, salt, and pepper in a bowl. Taste to make sure that it is seasoned to suit you; set aside.

In a straight-sided saucepan, heat the oil to 365°. The oil should be deep enough to float the oysters. If you don't have a thermometer, you can test the oil temperature with fair accuracy by dropping a little of the breading in it. If it sizzles, the oil is ready. Drain the oysters.

Working in batches so as not to crowd the oysters in either the breading bowl or the frying pan, toss the oysters in the breading and then transfer them to the oil. Fry for a minute to a minute and a half at most. They should float and be pretty and brown when done. Let the oil recover its heat between batches. Drain the oysters in a bowl lined with a clean kitchen towel, then dust with sea salt.

Serve at once with lemon wedges and a favorite sauce.

Out in the Yard

Roasted Oysters and Hard-Crab Stew are messy and thus are summertime meals that my family always served outdoors. You can of course bring them both inside if you like. I've include instructions for cooking the oysters either place. The crab stew is cooked indoors, wherever you choose to eat it.

Roasted Oysters

The oyster roast is a tradition all along the coastal South, and I've attended them my whole life. This isn't so much a recipe as it is a procedure, and a free-form procedure at that. Although big oyster parties are generally outdoor affairs, it is quite possible to roast oysters in the kitchen oven, so I've included instructions for cooking them in either place. The same sauces used for raw oysters all work well with roasted ones.

SERVES AS MANY AS YOU'D LIKE

At least 12 large oysters per person
Basic Cocktail Sauce (recipe follows)
Basquaise Sauce (page 23)
Lemons and horseradish

You must first clean the shells. It is rare to receive oysters that couldn't use one more scrubbing. In the yard with a garden hose is the most effective, but if that isn't possible, the sink will do. Submerge the oysters in cool water to loosen the dirt, but remember that they won't like fresh chlorinated water. Left too long, they will probably die, in fact, so after a quick soak, rinse them under cold running water. Refrigerate them under damp cloths until you are ready to cook.

If you are cooking outside, you will need to prepare a fire and let it burn down to glowing coals. This can be done in your outdoor grill. We always used wood growing up, but in recent years I have seen charcoal used successfully. Again, when I was growing up, there was always a sheet of corrugated metal around to serve as a roasting pan. You can use any baking sheet or roasting pan for this, but keep in mind that they may warp on the fire, so you may want to use something that is already old and beat up. Place the oysters on the pan and cover with wet cloth. If the oysters came in a burlap bag, rinse it out and use it. It will be perfect. Cooking time will vary because of the size of the oysters and the amount of time they have been out of the sea. They are ready when they have just *barely* begun to open. People will need to be careful retrieving these from the fire. It might be a good idea to have one person in charge of this.

If you are going to do this inside, preheat your oven to high (500° in most ovens) or broil. Have your guests assembled. Place the oysters on sheet pans in single layers and cover with wet cloth. Put the oysters in the oven. Start looking at them after 8–10 minutes. People like different degrees of doneness. I like mine when they have just barely begun to open. They will be hot of course, but they don't hold well, so people will need to figure out how to handle them without getting burned. They always do. You can provide dish towels or oven mitts to help out, but these usually quickly become soaked with juice, causing diners to lose patience with them. Give everyone oyster knives and lead them to the sink. It's best to open oysters with the deeper side of the shell on the bottom, so you can drink the juices that will gather there.

Basic Cocktail Sauce

This is ready in about three seconds. You can adjust the amounts of horseradish or Tabasco sauce to suit your need for spiciness. This is also good with any kind of fried seafood.

MAKES 1 ½ CUPS

1 (10-ounce) jar commercial cocktail sauce
Juice of 1 lemon
2 tablespoons horseradish, or to taste
Dash of Tabasco sauce

Mix everything together and refrigerate until needed.

Hard-Crab Stew

Hard-crab stew is always a summer supper because it is so messy to eat that no one wants to serve it in the house. My grandmother only made it once or twice a year, and it was always a big deal. We always assemble at the newspaper-covered picnic table to eat this. All the shells could be rolled up and taken to the trash when we were through. This is the second version of this recipe that I have published. The first was one I found among my grandmother's things after she died. It was in her handwriting, but it wasn't quite what I remembered. Recently, a new version has surfaced. It was given to me by an old friend of the family who had been given it years ago, again in Grandmother's handwriting. Needless to say, this discovery sent a ripple of disbelief through the family ("it was in her *handwriting!"), but this newer version seems like the ur-stew to me.*

There is a common variation of this recipe where the bread is omitted and replaced by white cornmeal dumplings. Some of the dumplings are broken up into the stew to thicken it, so no cornmeal is stirred in at the end. I've included a recipe for the dumplings below. Be warned. You will be eating this stew mostly with your hands. Claw crackers would be handy. (We used to get yelled at for cracking the claws with our teeth.)

SERVES A CROWD

½ pound side meat or fatback
2 medium onions, peeled and cut into large dice
2 dozen hard crabs, cleaned and halved
½ teaspoon crushed red pepper flakes
4 bay leaves
1 teaspoon dried thyme
6 baking-size potatoes, peeled and cut into eighths

¾ cup all-purpose cornmeal, stirred into 2 cups of cold water
and shaken in a mason jar
Salt and black pepper, to taste
Sliced white bread or Cornmeal Dumplings (recipe follows)

Render the side meat in a large stockpot. Do this slowly on low heat, as it has a low smoking point and you want to extract as much fat as possible before it gets too brown. It will resemble crisp bacon in color when ready. Add the onions and sauté until soft but not brown. Add the crabs and cover with cold water. Add the red pepper, bay leaves, and thyme. Bring to a boil, reduce the heat and simmer for half an hour.

Add the potatoes and cook until they are well-done, 15–20 minutes more. Turn up the heat a little (but you don't want a hard boil) and stir in the cornmeal and water. (Omit this step if you are using the dumpling variation.) This will be a little difficult because of the crabs. You need to mix this in thoroughly. Bring back to a simmer until the stew begins to thicken.

If you are using dumplings, now is the time to add them. Tuck them around the edge of the pot and spoon a little of the soup over each one from time to time. Season the stew with salt and pepper, keeping in mind that some side meat is saltier than others. To serve, ladle into large soup bowls, giving everyone crabs, a few dumplings, and potatoes.

To serve without dumplings, put a slice or two of white bread in the bottom of large soup bowls and ladle the stew, crabs and all, on top.

Cornmeal Dumplings

These are dense, unleavened dumplings. My great grandmother also cooked them on top of her collards.

MAKES 12 DUMPLINGS

2 cups white cornmeal
⅔ cups all-purpose flour
1 teaspoon salt
1¼ cups water

Sift the dry ingredients together into a large bowl, then completely mix in the water. With wet hands, divide the dough into twelve equal portions and form each into an oval-shaped dumpling. Place them around the edges of the stew pot for the last 20 or so minutes of cooking. Spoon the stew over the tops from time to time. Gently stir the stew to keep the dumplings from sticking, and break up a few of them with the spoon.

Dinnertime

Travel often leads to adventures at the dinner table, and all this talk of supper makes me remember a trip to Japan. There is a wonderful restaurant in the Gion district of Kyoto called Kappa Nawate. It's basically a lunch counter surrounding a grill on three sides. It is small, crowded, loud, and merry. I had already eaten a great deal there when I noticed an enormous red crab sitting in a display case. I pointed to it, not realizing that I would be served the whole thing. The preparation is elaborate. It ends with sake being boiled in the carapace. You drink this like soup. Then the cook tells you that you must chew on this mesh of brown fibers with red dots that is found behind the eyes. When in Rome. . . . It was delicious.

This section actually begins with one recipe that is served with main courses—oyster dressing. It's generally served at holidays alongside a turkey or a ham. All the others are main courses. A few are peculiar, but that is deliberate. To me the cultural and the culinary are inseparable, and I wanted this book to illustrate both. The biscuits that are used with the oyster shortcake are delicious with other things as well.

Oyster Dressing

Someone in my family must not have liked this. It's a favorite holiday side dish everywhere, but, to my memory, we never were served it. Therefore it was a pleasure to try this out. I tried this once with crumbled stale cornbread instead of white bread. It was good but a little less solid.

MAKES A GENEROUS QUART

1 stick unsalted butter

5 celery stalks, sliced thinly

1 medium onion, chopped medium

3 cups cubed and toasted white bread

$\frac{1}{4}$ cup chopped fresh parsley

$\frac{1}{2}$ teaspoon salt

$\frac{1}{4}$ teaspoon black pepper

$\frac{1}{2}$ teaspoon dried sage

$\frac{1}{2}$ teaspoon dried thyme

2 eggs, well beaten

1 pint shucked standard oysters, drained

Preheat the oven to 350°.

Melt the butter in a skillet and sauté the vegetables to soften but not brown. Pour the contents of the skillet into a large bowl and combine with the bread and all the herbs and seasonings. Fold in the eggs and oysters. Let it sit a minute so the bread can absorb the moisture. Spread evenly in a buttered baking dish and bake for about 20 minutes or until brown on top and firm at the center.

Deviled Crabs

I think that there are probably as many recipes for deviled crabs as there are cooks who make them. They are the potato salad of seafood. They are also the first crabs that I clearly remember. I grew up on these. They are essentially a crab cake that has been baked in a crab shell. I went through a stack of church cookbooks to pull together this recipe. Different people have different ideas about what deviled means and about how much of it they want. I found some recipes that called for the tiniest amount of seasoning that I've ever seen. I was raised to believe that deviled meant spicy, but this spice comes from mustard rather than chilies. I did find one with horseradish, but the heat baked out of it and it tasted sour. I didn't like it.

Growing up, we caught and picked most of our crab so we always had shells to stuff. If you're not doing that and don't live near the coast where you might be able to buy some, use buttered, four-ounce porcelain or glass baking ramekins.

MAKES 8–12 SERVINGS, DEPENDING ON
THE SIZE OF THE CRAB BACKS YOU HAVE

1 pound fresh back fin crabmeat, picked over for shell
¾ teaspoon salt
2 tablespoons unsalted butter
1 small green bell pepper, diced (about 1 cup)
12 saltine crackers, crumbled, plus a few more to
   sprinkle on top
2 tablespoons yellow mustard
3 tablespoons mayonnaise
¼ cup cider vinegar
½ teaspoon Tabasco sauce
1 tablespoon Worcestershire sauce
2 tablespoons fresh lemon juice
2 tablespoons cold unsalted butter

Preheat the oven to 375°. If you are not using crab backs, butter 8–12 ramekins.

In a large bowl, toss the crabmeat with the salt and let rest for 10 minutes. Melt the butter in a skillet, add the bell peppers, and sauté just until soft. Pour off the excess butter. Add the cracker crumbs to the crabmeat and toss to combine; stir in the green peppers. In a separate bowl, mix the mustard, mayonnaise, and vinegar together with the seasonings, then fold this into the crab.

Fill the crab backs (or ramekins) with the crab mixture. Sprinkle with more cracker crumbs and dot with the cold butter. Bake for about 15 minutes or until hot at the center. The time required will vary some according to what they're cooked in. Crab shells are very thin and will thus heat through more quickly than china ramekins. Serve at once.

Jean Anderson's Stuffed Crab au Gratin
Santola Recheada a Gratinada

I love Portugal. Jean Anderson is absolutely nuts about it. Luckily for me, when this talented and remarkably prolific cookbook author decided to move back home to North Carolina, she came to Chapel Hill. We've become friends, sharing the occasional dinner or food-themed excursion. This recipe comes from her classic cookbook The Food of Portugal *(first published in 1986). This recipe struck me as perhaps a cousin of our North Carolina–style deviled crab. I especially love the black olives.*

MAKES 6 SERVINGS

1 medium yellow onion, peeled and finely chopped

1 medium carrot, peeled and finely chopped

⅓ cup finely chopped sweet red peppers

1 tablespoon olive oil

1 tablespoon unsalted butter

2 tablespoons water

1 pound fresh lump crabmeat, picked over for shell,
   then flaked

1¼ cups moderately fine soft white bread crumbs, divided

⅓ cup mayonnaise

3 tablespoons chopped oil-cured black olives

3 tablespoons tawny port

3 tablespoons light cream or half-and-half

1 tablespoon Dijon mustard

1 tablespoon fresh lemon juice

1 tablespoon minced fresh parsley

½ teaspoon salt

¼ teaspoon hot red pepper sauce

⅛ teaspoon black pepper

2 tablespoons grated Parmesan cheese

Preheat the oven to 400°.

In a small heavy skillet over moderate heat, sauté the onions, carrots, and red peppers in the butter and oil for about 2 minutes. Add the water and cover, then turn down the heat as low as possible and let steam for 15 minutes.

Meanwhile, place ½ cup of the bread crumbs and the rest of the ingredients, minus the cheese, in a large bowl and toss lightly to mix. Add the skillet's contents and mix well. Mound into crab backs or buttered 5- to 6-ounce ramekins. Combine the remaining bread crumbs with the cheese and sprinkle on top of the crabs. Bake, uncovered, for about 20 minutes. The tops should brown a little.

Crab and Oyster Gumbo

I suspect that every family in Louisiana has its own recipe for gumbo. This is a version of the one that we use at Crook's Corner. Almost every kind of meat or seafood can appear in gumbo, so say you have a handful of leftover breakfast sausage with no home, for example, you can crumble that in.

SERVES A CROWD

12 tablespoons unsalted butter
2 cups all-purpose flour
1 small whole chicken (3 pounds or so)
1 cup diced side meat or bacon
4 cups diced onions
4 cups diced green bell peppers
½ pound andouille (or some other sausage that you like),
    sliced into ¼-inch rounds
2 tablespoons chopped garlic
1 (28-ounce) can crushed tomatoes
4 bay leaves
½ teaspoon crushed red pepper flakes
½ teaspoon dried thyme
½ teaspoon dried oregano
½ teaspoon dried basil
1 pound sliced okra (fresh is great, but frozen is fine and
    comes in 1-pound bags)
Salt and black pepper, to taste
1 pound fresh special crabmeat, picked over for shell
2 pints shucked oysters
Cooked rice

Preheat the oven to 350°.

Melt the butter in a cast-iron skillet. Whisk in the flour until completely incorporated. Stir constantly until the roux has taken on the color of peanut butter. Put the skillet in the oven and bake for 45 minutes or so, stirring from time to time, or until the roux is the color of almost-burnt toast. It can get quite dark before it begins to taste burned. Remove from the oven and let it rest for half an hour. Pour off any oil that has collected on the top. Set aside. (You can do this part days in advance. Just re-warm the roux when you are ready to resume cooking.)

Bring a large pot of water to a boil (there should be enough water to float the chicken). Add the chicken and return to a boil. Cook for 15 minutes, then turn off the heat and let the chicken sit for 20 minutes more. Remove the chicken from the pot and refrigerate. When its cool enough to touch, pick the meat from the carcass and return the meat to the refrigerator. Throw the skin and bones back into the stock and bring to a hard boil. Boil for 1 hour and then strain the stock into another pot to cool a bit and to settle. This will also give you the opportunity to degrease the stock. (You don't have to remove every speck of grease, by the way.)

Render the side meat or bacon in a heavy-bottomed soup pot until you have some grease. Add the and onions and bell pep-pers and sauté until soft. Add the andouille and cook for 5 or so minutes. If things brown a little, that's fine. Stir in the garlic. Cook for 3 minutes, then add the tomatoes and 4 cups of the strained chicken stock. Keep in mind that you may have to add more of the stock or water later. Bring to a simmer and add the seasonings. Simmer for 45 minutes, stirring from time to time.

Fold the warm roux, bit by bit, into the gumbo. You will need to stir this often since the flour tends to sink and is easy to scorch. Bring to a simmer and add the okra and chicken. Cook until the okra is done, about 10 minutes more. Taste for salt and pepper. At serving time, fold in the crabmeat and oysters. Cook just until the oysters begin to curl. Serve at once in large bowls over a scoop of rice.

Stuffed Crabs

I came upon this recipe on a second pass through that fantastic cookbook from the Brookhaven Junior Auxiliary. It is in effect an un-deviled crab. The interesting thing here is the use of egg yolks creamed into whole butter as a thickener.

FILLS 10 CRAB BACKS

2 tablespoons unsalted butter
1 tablespoon bacon grease
½ cup finely chopped green bell peppers
½ cup finely chopped celery
2 cups heavy cream
3 tablespoons unsalted butter, softened
2 egg yolks
½ teaspoon paprika
1 tablespoon fresh lemon juice
1 pound fresh crabmeat (grade of your choice),
    picked over for shell
1 cup toasted bread crumbs, plus more to dust the tops
Melted unsalted butter to baste the crabs

Preheat the oven to 400°.

Heat the butter and grease in a skillet; add the bell peppers and celery and sauté until soft. Add the cream and bring to a simmer. Cream the butter, egg yolks, and paprika together with a fork until smooth and stir into the simmering cream until it thickens. Do not boil. Add the lemon juice, then the crabmeat. Simmer for a minute or two more, stirring constantly. Fold in the bread crumbs.

Fill the crabs shells, dust with more bread crumbs, and drizzle with a little melted butter. Bake for 20 minutes to warm through. Serve at once.

Crabes Farcis

This must be the Louisiana version of the stuffed crabs from Mississippi. They share that strange ingredient of egg yolks creamed into butter, which I don't recall ever seeing before this project, only this time the egg yolk has been boiled. I was surprised by how much I liked this. It is so much less rich than so many of these recipes are, and I love all of the garlic.

MAKES 6 SERVINGS

---

12 large crabs, boiled in salted water, or 1 pound fresh
    back fin crabmeat, picked over for shell
1 tablespoon unsalted butter
3 hard-boiled eggs, yolks and whites separated
3 garlic cloves, minced
2 tablespoons chopped fresh parsley
Zest and juice of 1 lemon, divided
2 tablespoons dry sherry
2 tablespoons bread crumbs
Lemon wedges

Preheat the oven to 350°.

If you have boiled your own crabs, carefully pick the meat and save the 6 prettiest backs; set aside. If you are not using crab backs, butter 6 ramekins.

In a small bowl, mash the butter and egg yolks together. Rough chop the egg whites and place in large bowl. Add the crabmeat, garlic, parsley, lemon zest, sherry, and butter-and-egg-yolk paste and stir until well combined.

Fill the crab backs (or ramekins), dust tops with bread crumbs, and squeeze the lemon over them all. Bake for 15–20 minutes. (Ramekins take a little longer than crab backs to heat through.) Serve hot with lemon wedges.

Soft-Shell Crabs

I like to serve two medium-size crabs per person. At Crook's, I generally order primes, which is the middle classification of five (see page 6). They fall between hotels and jumbos. Over the years I've switched from cornmeal, to corn flour, to Maseca for my seafood breading. Maseca is the corn flour ground to make tamales.

MAKES 4 SERVINGS

---

8 cleaned soft-shell crabs

2 cups buttermilk

2 cups self-rising flour

2 cups Maseca

½ teaspoon salt

¼ teaspoon black pepper

½ cup clarified butter or cooking oil

1 stick unsalted butter

4 tablespoons chopped garlic

¼ cup fresh lemon juice

½ cup finely shredded basil leaves

Place the buttermilk in a large bowl and submerge the crabs in it. In a separate bowl, combine the flour, Maseca, salt, and pepper. In a large skillet over high heat, heat enough butter or oil to cover the bottom by ¼ inch. (You don't want to crowd the crabs as they cook or they won't be crisp, so cook them in batches if need be, adding more butter or oil as you go. The cooked crabs may be held in a warm oven while you finish a batch.) When the oil begins to shimmer, working with one crab at a time, remove them from the buttermilk, shake off the excess, put them in the flour to coat completely, and shake off the excess as well. Place as many of the crabs into the pan as you can, shell side down, without crowding. They should sizzle at once. Cook for 3 or 4 minutes on one side or until brown, then flip each crab and brown the other side. If the crabs are browning too quickly, you may need to turn the heat down a little at this point, but you still want the sizzle. As the crabs are brown and clearly cooked through, move them to a serving platter and put in a warm oven. You may need to wipe the pan between batches if there is a lot of dark breading.

When all the crabs have been cooked and are in the warm oven, wipe the pan clean and return it to high heat. Toss in the whole butter and swirl the pan as it melts. In a minute or two it will begin to brown and to smell sort of toasty. Throw in all of the garlic and swirl without ceasing. Cook just until the garlic starts to turn brown. Add the lemon juice and basil and stir to combine. Pour the sauce over the crabs and serve at once.

Crabmeat Cobbler

I got the idea for this recipe in a mysterious, coverless ring-bound collection that my father had. It is attributed to someone named Jay Lippitt, a person unknown to me. I had never seen a seafood cobbler before, and even more intriguing, the crust appeared to be old-fashioned drop cheese biscuits. What's more, the onions are cooked in a double boiler rather than sautéed. My first attempt produced something that resembled a particularly good tuna casserole. After several testings, I came up with this sort of potpie interpretation.

MAKES 6–8 SERVINGS

FOR THE FILLING

24 pearl onions
1 stick unsalted butter
½ cup chopped onions
½ cup sifted all-purpose flour
1 teaspoon dry mustard
1 cup milk
1 cup shredded cheddar cheese
3 hard-boiled eggs, chopped
1 cup crabmeat
1½ cups drained diced tomatoes (fresh are good in season, otherwise use canned)
2 teaspoons Worcestershire sauce
½ teaspoon salt

1 cup all-purpose flour
2 teaspoons baking powder
½ teaspoon salt
¼ cup shredded cheddar cheese
2 tablespoons shortening, lard, or butter
½ cup milk

Preheat the oven to 450°. Cut off the root ends of the pearl onions and toss into boiling salted water for a few seconds. Transfer to ice water, then peel; set aside.

Melt the butter in a double boiler; add the chopped onions and cook until tender, about 10 minutes. Combine the flour and mustard and stir into the onions. Follow with the milk, then the cheese. Cook, stirring constantly, until thick. Fold in the pearl onions, eggs, crabmeat, tomatoes, Worcestershire sauce, and salt and pour into a 2-quart casserole.

Start the crust by sifting together the dry ingredients. Using 2 forks, thoroughly blend in first the shortening and then the cheese. Gradually stir in the milk, but add only enough to moisten the flour (you may not need the entire ½ cup).

Drop the batter with a soup spoon over the top of the warm crab mixture. (You don't need to cover every square inch with crust.) Bake until brown and bubbly around the edges, about 20 minutes.

Oyster Shortcake

This recipe makes use of an old-fashioned thickening technique—beurre manié, where butter is rubbed into flour, then whisked into hot liquids. The dish is sort of an oyster stew on toast. It calls for just four biscuits, but since there's no such thing as extra biscuits, the recipe here, which makes about twelve, will do nicely. You can also freeze the unused dough and use it for fried croutons. I used leftover biscuits for this, because we often have them at work.

MAKES 4 SERVINGS

FOR THE BISCUITS

2 cups self-rising flour

4 tablespoons cold unsalted butter, diced

¾ cup buttermilk

FOR THE OYSTERS

1 pint shucked oysters, drained, juice reserved

1½ cups milk

3 teaspoons unsalted butter

3 tablespoons all-purpose flour

Salt and cayenne pepper, to taste

Preheat the oven to 375°.

To make the biscuits, cut the butter into the flour until completely blended. I use two forks. Stir in just enough buttermilk to form a dough that is a little sticky but pulls away from the mixing bowl (you may need more or less than ¾ cup). Turn out the dough onto a floured surface and roll out to ½ inch with a floured rolling pin. Cut with a biscuit cutter. Put on a baking sheet, close together but not touching, and bake for 15 minutes or until pretty and brown. Remove from the oven and turn down the oven temperature to 350°. Return the biscuits to the oven to keep warm.

To prepare the oysters, in a small saucepan, scald the oyster juice and set aside. In another small saucepan, set the milk to simmer. In a bowl, using your fingers, rub the butter and flour together to form a paste. Whisk the mixture into the simmering milk and cook until it begins to thicken. Stir ¼ cup of the milk mixture into the oyster juice, then strain this back into the saucepan of milk. Continue to cook until rethickened. It will be a little thinner than gravy.

Stir the oysters into the milk and cook just until they begin to curl. Split 4 of the biscuits and put on individual plates. Layer the oysters and sauce between the biscuit slices and serve at once.

My Grandmother's Crab Pilaf

I have to say first of all that I have absolutely no memory of having been served this. I found it in my father's recipe collection and altered it a tiny bit. The inclusion of salted peanuts made it irresistible.

MAKES 4 SERVINGS

---

6 tablespoon vegetable oil

1 small onion, halved and thinly sliced

1 medium green bell pepper, halved, seeded, and cut into
   1/4-inch strips

2 celery stalks, thinly sliced

3 cups cold cooked rice

1/2 pound fresh special crabmeat, picked over for shell

1/4 cup salted peanuts

Soy sauce

Heat 4 tablespoons of the oil in a large frying pan. Add the vegetables and sauté until cooked but still a bit crisp, 5–6 minutes. Remove them from the pan. Heat the rest of the oil in the pan over medium heat. Add the rice and cook, stirring, until the grains separate. Return the vegetables to the pan and toss with the rice, followed by the crab and the peanuts. Cook to heat through. Serve in soup bowls accompanied by soy sauce.

Oyster Loaf, or Bread Box

This is a very peculiar recipe, and if it hadn't shown up in seafood cookbooks so often, I probably wouldn't have included it. I found many variations from all over. The common thread is the loaf of bread. When I first saw this mentioned, I assumed that it would be something like a meatloaf. This is nothing at all like a meatloaf.

MAKES 6–8 SERVINGS

1 loaf unsliced bread
Melted unsalted butter
1 pint (2 dozen or so) Fried Oysters (page 56)
1 large dill pickle, thinly sliced into rounds
1 lemon, thinly sliced into rounds
½ cup ketchup

Preheat the oven to 350°.

Slice the top off of the loaf of bread. Cut down into the loaf about a half an inch in on all four sides to a half an inch from the bottom, being careful not to pierce the opposite side. Remove the center of the loaf and cut off a ½-inch slice lengthwise. Paint both sides of the slice and the loaf, inside and out, with butter. Place on a cookie sheet and bake until lightly browned and crispy, 12–15 minutes.

Turn the oven down to 300°. Arrange half each of the oysters, pickles, and lemon in the bottom of the loaf. Sprinkle with half of the ketchup. Place the toasted slice on top and then another oyster, pickle, lemon, and ketchup layer. Return the top of the loaf to its place. Bake for 30 minutes. I'm not sure how you are supposed to serve and eat this. In my kitchen, we just stood around it and went at it with spoons.

Crab Soufflé

Finally a recipe containing canned soup! This recipe was on the back of an envelope that I found in a second-hand cookbook that someone brought me from Louisiana a million years ago. This is actually a rather elegant little dish. You need to serve it the minute it comes out of the oven as it becomes greasy with age. I'm always interested when recipes call for shortening or "cooking oil" instead of butter or lard. There was no mention of either what to cook this in or at what temperature. I used a porcelain pâté terrine that I buttered and lined with parchment because that is what I had on hand. The first time I made this, I set the terrine in a shallow pan of hot water that I had waiting in the oven. This is how one ordinarily cooks soufflés, but it refused to get done at the center and got too brown on top. A soufflé dish would obviously be appropriate. The batter has a volume of around five cups. This is so rich it doesn't really need any sauce, but a little sour cream might be nice on top of each serving.

MAKES 4 OR 5 SERVINGS

4 eggs, separated, at room temperature
1 cup milk
¼ teaspoon salt
⅛ teaspoon cayenne pepper
1 cup canned tomato soup
2 tablespoons cooking oil
1 small yellow onion, finely chopped
1 teaspoon curry powder
1 tablespoon all-purpose flour
1 cup cooked rice
1 cup fresh crabmeat, picked over for shell
A splash of cider vinegar, a pinch of salt, and a speck of
    cream of tartar
Sour cream (optional)

Preheat the oven to 375°. Butter a 6-cup soufflé dish; set aside.

In a large mixing bowl, beat the egg yolks, milk, seasonings, and tomato soup together well; set aside. In a large sauté pan cook the onion in the oil until soft but not brown. Whisk in the curry and allow to cook for a minute. Whisk in the flour, stirring until all of the lumps are gone (this is easier if you shake the flour into the pan with a kitchen sieve). Slowly stir the egg yolk mixture into the onions. Lower the heat and stir constantly until the liquid begins to thicken. Fold in the rice and the crab; set aside away from the heat.

Rinse the mixing bowl with the vinegar and dust it with salt. Swirl the bowl around and dump it out in the sink. Add the egg whites and the cream of tartar and beat to soft peaks. Fold the egg whites by thirds into the crab and transfer to the baking dish. Bake for 40 minutes or until the top is a little brown and a knife blade inserted into the center comes out clean. Serve at once.

Baked Crab Sandwiches

This recipe comes from my cousin Linda Morris. I discovered it while searching through a cookbook called Pass the Plate, *published by Christ Episcopal Church in my hometown of New Bern. I say discovered because since Linda is not an Episcopalian, I hadn't expected to find her among the contributors. Upon further reading, I realized that the women of that church had invited other congregations in town to join them, making the book a New Bern–wide effort. The results of the recipe vary according to the type of bread used. The first time I tried this I had a thin sliced brioche at work, which proved to be too small for the amount of custard in the original text. I've altered the instructions a little.*

MAKES 8–10 SERVINGS

12 slices sandwich bread, trimmed of crust if you like,
   buttered
½ pound fresh special crabmeat, picked over for shell
½ cup grated sharp cheddar cheese
3 cups milk
½ teaspoon curry powder
4 eggs, beaten
½ teaspoon salt

Preheat the oven to 325°.

Place 6 of the slices of bread, buttered side up, in the bottom of a 9 × 12-inch baking dish. Spread the crabmeat evenly on top. Cover with the rest of the bread, again buttered side up. Distribute the cheese over the bread.

In a medium bowl, beat the curry into the milk until there are no lumps, then stir in the eggs and salt. Carefully pour half of this over the sandwiches. Wait 5 minutes for it to be absorbed. The bread should absorb all that you add and look wet but not be swimming (you might not need all of the rest of the egg mixture). Cover and refrigerate for at least 2 hours. (This can be done a day ahead and allowed to sit overnight.) Bake for 45 minutes or until the egg is set at the center and the top is pretty and brown.

Oyster Rarebit

Rarebits are really just melted cheese poured over toast. My aunt Hi used to make what she called Welsh rarebit from time to time. They did it to amuse me as much as anything, because I always called it "rabbit." I remember that she and her husband were unenthusiastic about the dish. I was little then, and although I knew that people ate rabbits, I was relieved that there were none in this. In this version the bunny has been replaced with sea creatures.

MAKES 4 SERVINGS

1 cup shucked oysters with their juice
2 eggs, well beaten
Scant ½ cup heavy cream
½ pound grated sharp cheddar cheese
⅛ teaspoon cayenne
Freshly grated nutmeg
Salt and black pepper, to taste
3 slices sandwich bread, toasted, buttered, and
    cut into triangles

Strain the oysters and beat their juice thoroughly into the eggs. Heat the cream in a saucepan, then whisk in the cheese until melted and thoroughly blended. (This is a little tricky, but just keep the cheese moving.) Then quickly add the egg mixture, followed by the cayenne and a few scrapes of nutmeg. You are just thickening the sauce not making scrambled eggs, so keep the heat low. Add the oysters and juice and cook just until the oysters begin to curl, about 3 minutes max. If the oysters have made the sauce too runny, fish them out and reduce the sauce without them for a minute. Taste for salt and pepper. Some cheese is saltier than others. Have the toast arranged on four plates and divide the rarebit among them. Serve at once.

Frances and Ed Mayes's
Spaghetti with Lemon and Crab

I love the way Italy cooks. It's simple and often also quick. There is a lot of truth to that old saw about it being difficult to get a bad meal in Italy. In 2012 Ed and Frances Mayes published their perfectly wonderful Tuscan Sun Cookbook, *and they have kindly allowed me to reprise this recipe from it. In an aside they suggest that without the crab, this would be "perfect for the day after a crippling feast." Perhaps so, but try it with the crab first.*

SERVES 4–6

---

1 pound spaghetti
2 tablespoons extra-virgin olive oil
1 pound fresh crabmeat
¼ cup white wine
½ cup lemon juice
½ teaspoon salt
¼ teaspoon black pepper
½ cup grated Parmigiano-Reggiano
½ cup chopped flat-leaf parsley

Cook the pasta in boiling salted water as directed. While the pasta cooks, heat the olive oil in a large skillet over low heat and cook the crabmeat just to warm it. Add the wine, bring it quickly to a boil, then immediately turn the heat back to low. Stir in the lemon juice and the seasonings.

Drain the pasta, but reserve a little of the water. Pour the pasta into the pan with the crab. Toss in ¼ cup of the Parmigiano and the parsley. If the pasta needs more liquid, add a little of the reserved pasta water. Serve in bowls, sprinkling the remaining cheese on top.

Green Cabbage Slaw

I am a big fan of slaw and have many favorite recipes. It is for this reason that I have dubbed this one Green Cabbage Slaw. I also make carrot slaw or my grandmother's mustard slaw, and at Crook's Corner we serve a red cabbage slaw. We developed this at work at about the same time as I was rediscovering grated onions, a useful but overlooked ingredient.

MAKES ABOUT 2 QUARTS

2 heads green cabbage, trimmed, cored, and quartered
1 medium onion, peeled and quartered
2 green bell peppers, stemmed, seeded, and quartered
6 carrots, peeled
½ tablespoon salt
¼ cup mayonnaise
1 cup cider vinegar
1 teaspoon dry mustard
½ cup sugar
Salt and black pepper, to taste

Grate the cabbage, onions, bell peppers, and carrots in a food processor using the coarser blade. Mix all together, squeezing as you do. Stir in the salt, which will accelerate juicing, and place the vegetables in a sieve to drain for 20 minutes.

Meanwhile, in a small bowl, whisk together the mayonnaise, vinegar, mustard, and sugar.

Squeeze the vegetables really well one last time and transfer to a bowl. Add the dressing and combine well. Season with salt and pepper. Remember that the salt you added earlier will still be present. Chill.

Two Kinds of Crab Cakes

There seem to be two schools of thought on crab cakes. One says they should be bound with beaten egg, while the other says they should be bound, oddly to me, with mayonnaise. I say oddly not because I don't approve of mayonnaise but because it doesn't seem like it would work. After some poking around, I decided to present one traditional version and one that is drifting toward Asia, and lo, both call for mayonnaise. My Cucumber Relish is an excellent dressing for both. If it appeals to you, make it before you begin the crab cakes, so that it can cure in the refrigerator and will be ready when the crab cakes are done.

Indochinese Crab Cakes

I found that frying these in daringly hot oil makes a great crust. If this spooks you, start the cooking in a frying pan and finish the cooking in a hot oven. The French brought mayonnaise to Indochina.

MAKES 5 OR 6 CRAB CAKES

Cucumber Relish (page 97)
3 tablespoons mayonnaise
1 tablespoon whole-grain mustard
2 teaspoons soy sauce
1 teaspoon fresh lemon juice
1 tablespoon chopped fresh parsley
1 teaspoon grated fresh ginger
1 teaspoon salt
½ teaspoon black pepper
Pinch or 2 of cayenne pepper
½ cup bread crumbs, or more as needed
1 pound fresh special crabmeat (but use a more expensive kind if you like), picked over for shell
½ cup clarified butter or cooking oil for frying (you might need more or less depending on the size of your pan)
Toasted sesame seeds (optional)

In a large bowl, mix the mayonnaise, mustard, and soy sauce together thoroughly. Add the lemon juice, all of the seasonings, and the bread crumbs. If the mixture seems suspiciously runny, add more crumbs. (The liquid in the ginger will be a factor in this. The mixture needs to be sticky enough to bind the crab.) Carefully fold in the crab and form into 5 or 6 cakes. Chill for an hour to let them set up.

Fry the crab cakes in the butter or oil for about 5 minutes on each side or until heated through. These won't brown as nicely as the other recipe. Serve with the Cucumber Relish and sprinkled with toasted sesame seeds, if using.

More Traditional Crab Cakes

When I was growing up I considered these the fried version of deviled crab. Recipes for both contain many of the same ingredients. Frying, of course, produces a much better crust than baking can.

MAKES 5 OR 6 CRAB CAKES

Cucumber Relish (page 97)
4 tablespoons unsalted butter, softened a little
⅓ cup chopped onion
3 slices dry, stale white bread, roughly crumbled
2 eggs, beaten
3 tablespoons mayonnaise
1 tablespoon yellow mustard
1 tablespoon Worcestershire sauce
½ teaspoon salt
½ cup clarified butter or cooking oil for frying (you might
    need more or less depending on the size of your pan)
1 pound fresh special crabmeat (but use a more expensive
    kind if you like), picked over for shell

In a large bowl, mix together the butter, onions, and bread. Fold in the eggs, mayonnaise, mustard, and Worcestershire sauce. Carefully fold in the crab and salt, keeping the meat intact as much as possible. Let the mixture rest for half an hour.

Form the crab mixture into 5 or 6 cakes and chill for an hour so they will set up. Fry in the butter or oil until pretty and brown, about 5 minutes on each side. Serve with the Cucumber Relish.

Cucumber Relish

This is a riff on something else I picked up in Mexico — a sort of cucumber slaw. Although it's not quite as clingy as tartar sauce or remoulade, it is a refreshing alternative to those mayonnaise-based sauces. Vary the amount of jalapeño to suit yourself.

MAKES ABOUT 2 CUPS

1 medium cucumber
½ cup minced red onions
1 tablespoon minced jalapeño
¼ teaspoon salt
¼ teaspoon black pepper
1 tablespoon chopped fresh parsley
1 tablespoon olive oil
2 teaspoon cider vinegar

If the peel on the cucumber is nice, leave it. Cut it into matchsticks and toss it with the other vegetables and the salt and pepper. Add the rest of the ingredients and chill for at least 20 minutes. Use as a sauce with crab cakes or other fried seafood.

Drinks

Indulge me here. When I first considered writing this book, almost the first thing that came to mind was a michelada with raw oysters that I had one glorious afternoon in Mexico City. A michelada is a drink. Trips to Mexico often have glorious moments, and this particular day began on top of the Pyramid of the Sun in Teotihuacan and ended in an evening of restaurant hopping in the neighborhood of Tlaxapana. As luck would have it, I came across the odd oyster juice tonic later in a pamphlet from before World War I, and thus a chapter on drinks was born.

Oyster Juice

I found this odd recipe for a tonic in Milady's Own Book, *a home-maker's pamphlet from the early nineteenth century. I didn't actu-ally try to make this, but I couldn't resist passing it along.*

"Oyster Juice is an excellent stimulant, but in itself contains little real nourishment. In preparing the oysters, care must be taken to scrub the shells absolutely clean. Place them in an enamel or earthenware dish, never in a tin one, with half a cup of cold water and put it in a hot oven. As soon as the shells open wide, take from the oven, drain all the juice from the shells and dish and strain into a cup that has been heated. Serve with long narrow slices of toast."

Two Micheladas with Oysters

Cervezas preparadas, or beer cocktails, are an acquired taste. Then all of a sudden you love them. One summer when I was in college I worked in Montana. People there drank beer mixed with tomato juice. Couldn't stand it. In Britain later on I was introduced to the shandy. Yuck. Then came a cold michelada in a hot, dusty outdoor market with a bunch of amigos in the town of Celaya in central Mexico. The michelada is a Mexican drink that's made by mixing beer with all kinds of things and served in a big, salt-rimmed goblet over ice. Recipes vary. They all call for lime juice and hot sauce. I've seen them with soy sauce and Worcestershire sauce, and some with that vegetable extract called Maggi. A version with soy sauce capped off a pretty much perfect day in Mexico City. It was full of raw oysters. Of course, after I had had a few of these came the second thoughts about eating raw oysters of unknown origins in places with spotty public health systems. This often happens to me when I'm traveling, though, when I get sort of swept up in the moment. I once polished off a very rare steak in a tiny town in the Ecuadorian Andes and I survived that too.

My friend Shannon Healy has a bar in downtown Durham, North Carolina, called Alley Twenty-Six. He kindly gave me an assist with this. The first recipe is for a standard version, the second is a fancier variation. They are both splendid with or without the oysters, but with them they make a sort of excellent liquid lunch. Modelo is the brand of Mexican beer much favored for michelada.

Putting the Tabasco on top of this drink gives it a great nose, and the first sip's combination of salty rim and spicy burn makes the drink go down fast. Tajín seasoning is a Mexican spice powder with dehydrated lime juice available at most tiendas; the mildest spice level is best here. If you can't find the Tajín brand, there are other comparable ones. If handy, some good mescal makes the fancy version of this drink delightfully smoky.

Michelada Tlaxapana

Half a lime, cut in quarters
Kosher salt
Tajín seasoning for rim of glass
1 (12-ounce) bottle Modelo Especial
¾ ounce tomato juice
½ ounce (by volume, use jigger) Tajín powder
½ ounce soy sauce
½ ounce fresh lime juice (from the lime quarters)
4 freshly shucked oysters, drained
Tabasco sauce

Moisten the lip of a chilled pint glass with a lime quarter. Roll the lip of the glass through a mixture of half kosher salt and half Tajín powder to coat. Fill the glass two-thirds of the way full with ice. Add 2 ounces of the beer. Add the tomato juice, Tajín powder, soy sauce, and lime juice. Stir in the oysters. Top with the remaining beer. Stir again. Float 3 dashes of Tabasco (or more, to taste) on top.

Michelada Tlaxapana Obscura

Half a lime, cut in quarters
Kosher salt
½ ounce (by volume, use jigger) Tajín seasoning,
    plus extra for the rim of the glass
Several dashes of cinnamon
1 (12-ounce) bottle Negro Model or other dark beer
¾ ounce tomato juice
½ ounce Worcestershire sauce
½ ounce fresh lime juice (from the lime quarters)
½ ounce mescal (optional)
4 freshly shucked oysters, drained
Tabasco sauce

Moisten the lip of a chilled pint glass with a lime quarter. Roll
the lip of the glass through a mixture of half kosher salt and half
Tajín powder and a dash of cinnamon to coat. Fill the glass two-
thirds of the way full with ice. Add 2 ounces of the beer. Add
the tomato juice, Tajín powder, a dash or two of cinnamon, the
Worcestershire sauce, the lime juice, and the mescal, if using.
Stir in the oysters. Top with the remaining beer. Stir again. Float
3 dashes of Tabasco (or more, to taste) on top.

Acknowledgments

I always say that the best thing about the food business is the collection of good friends and colleagues that comes along with it. I owe thanks to several of these folks, including Louis Osteen, Jean Anderson, Shannon Healy, and Ed and Frances Mayes, for allowing me to use their recipes. Thanks also to my cousin Linda Morris for her delicious Baked Crab Sandwiches recipe, to the membership of the Junior Auxiliary of Brookhaven, Mississippi, for several recipes and a sort of general inspiration, and to the Episcopal Diocese of East Carolina, which allowed me to quote from *Pass the Plate*, their splendid collection from the Episcopal Churchwomen of Christ Episcopal Church in New Bern, N.C. I'll be forever grateful to all of those people who contributed to church and community cookbooks all around the South. Thanks are due as well to Elaine Maisner, Alison Shay, and Mary Caviness of the University of North Carolina Press for all of their help, and I might add, patience, with this endeavor. Thanks also to Katharine Walton, my friend and agent, for constant encouragement. Finally, thanks to all of the cooks of my childhood who trained me to expect good food every time I sit down at the table.

Bibliography

Anderson, Jean. *The Food of Portugal*. New York: William Morrow, 1986.

Brookhaven Junior Auxiliary. *Cooks from Old Brook*. Brookhaven, Miss.: Brookhaven Junior Auxiliary, Inc., 1982.

Elie, Lolis Eric. *Treme: Stories and Recipes from the Heart of New Orleans*. San Francisco: Chronicle Books, 2013.

The Episcopal Churchwomen and Friends. *Pass the Plate*. Memphis: Wimmer Bros., 1981.

Mayes, Frances, and Edward Mayes. *The Tuscan Sun Cookbook: Recipes from Our Italian Kitchen*. New York: Clarkson Potter, 2012.

National Restaurant Association. *ServSafe CourseBook*. 5th ed. Upper Saddle River, N.J.: Prentice Hall, 2008.

Osteen, Louis. *Louis Osteen's Charleston Cuisine: Recipes from a Lowcountry Chef*. Chapel Hill, N.C.: Algonquin Books, 1999.

Root, Waverly. *The Encyclopedia of Food*. New York: Konecky & Konecky, 1980.

Index

Printed in the USA
CPSIA information can be obtained
at www.ICGtesting.com
CBHW081636180224
4434CB00013B/423

9 781469 677590